God's Measurements

OTHER BOOKS BY *Laurence Lieberman*

POETRY
The Unblinding
The Osprey Suicides

CRITICISM
The Achievement of James Dickey
Unassigned Frequencies: American
Poetry in Review (1964–77)

GOD'S MEASUREMENTS

Laurence Lieberman

LAURENCE LIEBERMAN

MACMILLAN PUBLISHING CO., INC.

NEW YORK

COLLIER MACMILLAN PUBLISHERS

LONDON

The following poems appeared originally in
The New Yorker: "Kimono," "God's Measurements,"
"The Washroom Ballet," and "Nara Park: Twilight
Deer Feeding."

Macmillan Publishing Co., Inc.
866 Third Avenue, New York, N.Y. 10022
Collier Macmillan Canada, Ltd.

Library of Congress Cataloging in Publication Data

Lieberman, Laurence.
    God's measurements.

    I. Title.
PS3562.I43G6   811'.5'4   79-25971
ISBN 0-02-069800-3

First Printing 1980

Printed in the United States of America

for my mother,
and in memory of
my father

Contents

Acknowledgments

I thank the editors of the following magazines, in which these poems first appeared:

American Poetry Review:	"The Sea Caves of Dogashima"
Back Door:	"Macaw and Parakeet"
Hudson Review:	"Flamingos of the Soda Lakes"
	"Joren: The Volcanic Falls"
	"Shakuhachi"
	"In Pursuit of the Angel"
Modern Poetry Studies:	"My Love Shooting the Buddha"
	"Lockjaw"
	"Riding the Duffle"
	"Two for the Evening Star"
	"The Beacon Light of Oshima"
The Nation:	"Blue Heron"
New England Review:	"Interview"
	"Yoshino: False Dawn of the Cherry Blossom"
The New Yorker:	"Kimono"
	"The Washroom Ballet"
	"God's Measurements"
	"Nara Park: Twilight Deer Feeding"
Partisan Review:	"The Kofukuji Arsonists"
Poetry:	"Daibutsu"
Sewanee Review:	"Wreckage of the Pagoda Moons"
South Carolina Review:	"Cape Iro: The Stone Pillars"
Sou'wester:	"The Human Bomb"
Yale Review:	"Shimoda: The Lava Shores"

I. In Pursuit of the Angel

KIMONO

Clonking up the cobbled roadway, I bob
And pitch on wood-slab clogs, my
Kimono sleazily mismatched under the twice-
Wrapped-round-my-middle sash. *Gaijin*, unkempt,
I halt, stopped by handmaiden's icy grace,
Who, with deft authority, ripping open
The dishevelled robes, unmasks my timid nudity.
A few swift tucks and shakes. The gown lies
Flat, seamless. Ah, maidservant, my bones
Go soft, collapsed and flattened, a hundred ribs
Smoothening under my soft silkskin.

THE WASHROOM BALLET

(Ise-Shima Youth Hostel)

Isaac and
   I, seated
      side by side
         on the cement-
slab ledge, are poised to brave the baths,
a hot steamy rectangle stretching from wall
         to wall below
            our dangled legs. . . . First, we enter

the crammed washroom,
      some ten or
         a dozen men
         and boys, stooped
and lolling thin necks, limbs ochre-
sallow in the steam, lemon-tinted
         in the shimmery
           fluorescence of salmon wall

tiles. Soaping
      and rinsing,
         they pour slow rivers
         from the small
buckets, runnels coursing down their backs—
lissome male torsos dipping and twisting,
         a slow-gestured,
         lingering ballet: prelude

to the baths.
      Others, doffing
         kimono-
         styled bathrobes,
pitch their cloaks over wall hooks, or
between high shelves, in the same loose-jointed
         gliding motion. . . .
         All figures are reflected

in two floor-to-
      ceiling mirrors,
         fore and aft,

doubling, quadrupling
the lean handsome midriffs—layer
upon layer of gyrating elbows, shoulders,
      bums—multiples
        of loin and flank dizzying

the sight: a jig-
      saw skinquilt,
        unbroken
        patchwork blent
in the mirrors' hypnotic cinema-
tography. Still others, washed and rinsed,
      shyly hiding
        their genitals behind towel,

sponge, bucket
      or bath cap,
        strive—on tiptoe—
        to elongate
their slim frames, narrowing hips
and thighs to avoid clouting their fellows'
      flesh-silk. Each
        graces his fellow skeleton's

rented upright
      share. To each
        his slim ration
        of cubic
inches. Oh slender wills trimmed down
to slenderer means—a wizardry of body
        spareness!
        A magic of flattening!

DAIBUTSU

"Do not handle or climb on statue. Some people
believe it is sacred and venerable object.
[Entrance to statue interior below, one flight
steps down stairs. Price ten yen.]"

—Kotokuin Temple, Kamakura

We are standing—
empedestaled—inside the God's
bronze head. Winding slowly up two
cramped narrow flights of stairs,
we have risen

spiralling into the great hollow
brain-vault, scaffolded into nirvana!
Tiptoeing onto the raised platform, our arms
outstretched, we place our feet with care—the steps
vertebrae of a two-story-high seated and cross-legged divinity's
spinal column. We run our fingertips along seams, marvelling
over wrist-thick welded sutures joining gray-olive-green
tarnished metal skull-plates. Ourselves surprised,
we are foreign bodies—transplants—

two queerly displaced
upright oblongs, giddy and pious.
Our tongues take root in the Buddha's
medulla oblongata; our timid
hushed voices,

magnified, bounce from wall to wall
of the vast cranial and thoracic echo-chambers:
God, statue & cathedral are of the one body, a hollow
clerestory in the church-nave of the colossus' shoulders.
Beginning our descent, we peer from the back through a single barred
window overlooking the sacred courtyard of the temple grounds—
burnt or beaten flat by fires and one great tidal wave
in this century leaving only the God intact,
though tinselled and ornamented

with sargassum, nori-
seaweed streamers, all manner of sea-
wrack, driftwood, roof-tiles, dishevelled
bed-linens, kimonos, draperies. . . .
Now we survey the wide.

loft within the concave vaulted breast.
I am startled by the spectral figure of a doll-
sized deity, miniature squat replica of the whale-Buddha
through which we navigate our Jonah rites of passage, supported
on a small platform in a shallow recess of the rib-cage wall opposite.
It stares up at us: no mere fetus, but a scaled-down midget God,
offspring with identical features of the parent colossus;
the tiny mirror-image figure no infant divinity
but an ingested surrogate mind's-eye,

interior guardian
of the great Daibutsu! We
have entered the grand divine corpus
and meet Him face-to-face
within His own body

chambers. Mother, you have come,
knowing my untold need. Together, taken
into the God's cavernous integument and dumbfounded
by his spellbinding eye, at once, we hover in the single
good lung—though it, too, failingly—that kept my father alive
for our last best ten family years, and the resounding
boom of the gong we hear is a great sigh my father
heaves with his one good lung ballooning
around us, coming back in the God's

barrel-chested breath.
Oh, I know that wheeze and rasp
of phlegm & the surpassing joy of each
forced-breath taken in love of us,
so sweet his ease of heart

with each pained insuck of air,
and we know ourselves lifted in my father's
four-years-bereft stertorous wind-bag, the pleura
membrane of his good lung pulsating, fluttering in the God's
embronzed thorax; and here, in this heaving peace of an unearthly
metal-alloy aspiration, inhaling our recombined newly dead,
we three are born again in the stale crypt-foul Orient
air of a mammoth acoustics chamber, amphi-
theater of eternal return.

GOD'S MEASUREMENTS
(Todaiji Temple, Nara)

"The statue weighs 452 tons, measures 53.5 ft. in height, and
has a face 16 ft. long by 9.5 ft. wide, eyes 3.9 ft. wide, a nose 1.6
ft. high, a mouth 3.7 ft. wide, ears 8.5 ft. long, hands 6.8 ft.
long, and thumbs 4.8 ft. long. The materials employed are
estimated as follows: 437 tons of bronze; 165 lbs. of mercury; 288
lbs. of pure gold; 7 tons of vegetable wax; and an amazing
amount of charcoal and other materials."

As incense smoke thins, a stupendous,
    wide, brooding face emerges above us. The long ribbon-looped
ears, ending in weighty teardrop-
    fat lobes, slowly unravel from the wrappings of smoke trails
    as we advance, the whole bronze olive-green head
        mushrooming from its mask
        of mist. It floats, hovers—balloonlike, isolate—
over the befogged shoulders. A cosmos
    of global body,
        seated cross-legged on a great lotus-
        blossom bronze pedestal, ascends

into the clearing before us,
    the pedestal in turn installed on a broader stone base
which knows touch of our hastily donned
    slippers, blocking our passage. Not one forward step possible,
    we backstep twice to see the more clearly
        over the jutting head-
        high edge of stone, the full figure now vivid
    and preternaturally clear before us,
        body draped in swirls
        of cloud, itself cloud-shaped, cloud-alloyed,
        growing into a mass, a solid—

if wavery—form. Still, it is the head,
    so distant, holds us. Why do we so thrill at eye-guessed
estimates of measurements, measurements!
    The eyes and mouth, wide as you are long, my son; the length
    of ears makes two of you, the height of lofty face
        three of me, and, yes,
        you could ride lying on the thumb, your near mate
    for length and width, the two of you nestled
        together mimicking
        a God's freakish double thumb! But, no, I
        will not lift you to the stone ledge,

launching your unstoppable climb
    to test my twin-thumbs caprice, despite your scandalous wails
reverberating in the temple
    upper chambers, strident in my ears; nor shall I scold
    or muzzle you, but hoist you to my shoulders
      where, first clasping hands
        for lift and support as you unfold to your full
        height above my head, I clench your ankles,
          as much to steady
            and balance you as to prevent surprise
            leaps. Together, of a tallness

to match, or exceed, the whole hand's length,
    let us promenade around His Excellency's right flank.
Now, wobblingly, we stalk: you, stiltjack,
    in love with instant towers sprung from the idiot body's
    endlessly stretchable elastic of flesh, I
      half scaffold, half anchor,
        the two of us a father-son hobbling hinge—
telescope of our bones, joined end to end,
      not doubled up
        in laughter or loss of balance but bending
        and unbending into beatitudes. . . .

We look up, to scrutinize the God, stilt-
    walking our charmed gavotte. Then, looking into each other's
      eyes—
I staring up, you staring down—
    we both shudder, communing between your flexed legs, spread
    the width of my two shoulders: our four eyes,
      riveted in silence,
        agree! We have seen the bronze head nod. The eyelids
flutter. The bronze bosom draw breath. The tarnished skins
    of metal wrinkling
      into folds over charcoal hid ribs. Organs—
      heart and lungs—of vegetable wax, waxen

liver, waxen pancreas. All glands,
    mercury, but in pure form, not poisons fed upon by dying
fish hordes. Our eyes swear we both saw
    bronze flesh breathe, bronze knees shift for comfort under all

that obese weight (no gold in the fat buttocks, fat
   hips, we agree to that!),
      grand flab he can never jog off in throes
of deep meditation. Does he diet, or fast?
   Does he shed bronze, gold,
         or weightless, sad wax only? We crane our necks
      to see how he leans and sways, as we wend

our wide, counterclockwise, happy circle
      around him, counting splendid curled petals of the great lotus-
blossom seat, the petals alternately
   pointing upward and curving downward, the puffed whirlwinds
of incense smoke eddying up, thinning out,
      in sudden gusts and lulls,
         as if the blossom itself exhaled the perfume
   clouds submerging all but the Ancient's head, breath
      after vaporous breath. . . .
         We revolve, degree by slow degree, circling
         the statue's base, half again wider

than the vast lotus throne half again
      the diameter of the bloated God's girth, and we behold
the thousand views of the Buddha's
   changing postures, the torso's bulk crafted by an army
of master sculptors. *Eight near-perfect castings*
   in three years. Aborted casts,
      unnumbered. No surmising how many dozens
   of failed castings, cracked one-hundred-foot-wide
   molds, collapsed scaffolds,
         casters of irreplaceable genius crushed
         in falling debris. . . . Sudden glare!

We squint, sun cascading into the hall
      from hidden windows high in the temple cupola—thousands
of sparkly points on the statue's
   coruscating skull flare on, off, on, off, and I can see
great circles connecting all dots of light
      on meticulously shaped
         rondures of annealed jaw plates, shoulder plates, breast
      plates, my sight travelling in arcs and swirls, curved
         lines running in a mesh
            of intersecting spirals dense as cross-
            hatching in the divinely crafted

anatomies of Hieronymus Bosch
> or the woodcut body dissections of Vesalius: God's
or human's, all the light-lines engraved
> on the celestial body's grandly continuous surface
> intersect. *Our body, a wing shining*
>> *in the happy, happy*
>>> *light of its wholeness. A moonlit angel's wing*
>> *in flight. Or underwater devil ray's*
>>> *wing torchlit*
>>>> *by diver's forehead searchlight beam. . . .*
>>> High throne-back behind the Buddha's

head usurps our view while we wind
> around his back side, topped not by headrest or flat cushion,
as it had appeared to us wrongly
> in profile, but a goldleaf-covered broad wooden halo
> decorated with portraits of sixteen Bosatsu,
>> by our ambulatory
>>> count, a troop of gilt sub-deities, satellites
>> in orbit perpetually—each a mirror,
>>> or reflecting moon,
>>>> to the one Daibutsu. . . . *Oh, look! The whole halo*
>>>> *is shimmering, dancing before our eyes!*

MY LOVE SHOOTING THE BUDDHA

No guide, nor host, nor escort—a mere fluffy-white-
turtlenecked and bescarfed
      tagalong—I
  saunter a few steps behind Mrs. Kubota, our pacemaker,
      wary of obtruding into the closed
        circle of ladies'
Tuesday hikes—that going enterprise! Never before have I,
in the outdoors company of nubile
    members of the female
Race, felt less a chaperone: I, the one led, not leading,
      helplessly swept along on the chatter
      of oceanic cama-
raderie. The eldest ladies—prancing from rock to rock
with the vim and gusto of nanny-
    goats, bowlegged,
displaying varicose calves—are the most nimble, spry climbers.
     We start trudging—single file—
      into the uphill wilds,
following a path often obscured by weeds. I get sidetracked
from the tour, quickly scaling
    the highest rocky
pinnacle anywhere in sight, easily finding footholds staggered
     in a zigzag upward spiralling
     path, hurl myself
to the top, teetering deliberately on the edge overhanging a sheer
sixty-foot dropoff. . . . *So. Today,*
    I can breathe. I
am open and take the gift of life—on rocks, cliffs, crags;
    but dread bridges, skyrise towers.
     The raw angularities
of rock, shifting and altering in slope, always wavering
like the poisons and panic within me,
    stand guard—life
answering to life's call for help: Gods in the rock, the weeds,
    reviving the self's Gods. . . . I glance
    across the abyss:
on the steep cliff-face opposite, a gentle life-giving Buddha—
etched deep in the rock, its cleanly
    moulded features
ultrahuman—stares back; those marbly-smooth limbs, so round,
    with the flowing, rotund indolence

of Renoir-breasts,
          lean to me, inviting me to find solace in their imperturbable
cool lines, to take my ease
          in a dreamy chill
     grace of upraised long rock-bones: elbows and wrists, fluid
               and sensual, arched like swans' wings
                    over the bald stone
     skull. Oh strange cliff-mother, Ok-san cut out of granite,
Mama-san, I reach out for your embrace!
     My arms outstretched,
     I step to the edge of the bluff to get a full, clear view
               of your waist, torso, hips—no,
                    I stand back aghast . . .
     behold! My beloved, reduced in scale to a minuscule pigmy,
stands at your cross-legged base
          aiming her Miranda
     zoom-lens diagonally across your chest, trajectory bisecting
               the loop of your earlobe which exceeds
                    in length her tiptoeing
     extended-skyward vertical skeleton. Your massive, stately figure
recedes into background, falls away
          to its true height,
     towering over the dwarfed, allured lady-sniper who adroitly mounts
               your right thigh, and lunging, boldly
                    hefts her trunk
     into your lap; many dangled shapes—camera, lenses, purse—
swinging from invisible straps
          slung round her neck.
     Ah, safe landing! . . . Lilliputian on the oriental Gulliveress'
               thighs, she wallows on all fours,
                    gets her balance;
     then, stabilizing on three points—one shoe-toe, one elbow, one
knee: forming a rude tripod, asway—
          she raises the camera
     to her eyes. Focuses. Refocuses. To my oblique eye-level, blinks
               of flashbulbs are glares emitted
                    by the Buddha's eyes,
     two pools of light raining waterfalls of sudden radiance
on my love's dishevelled, glistening
          bangs. Inspired, she warms
     to her work, replacing rolls of film, changing lenses, dancing
               round the cavernous shelf housing
                    the stone Goddess,

wedging herself between its flanks and the shallow-cave walls to
win
an upslanting profile of the bust—
        head, neck & shoulder—
        success: "Gorgeous shots, Bravo!" I nearly shout, but I'm mute,
             stunned into silence by the glory
                of her art in solitude—
bestowals of her womanly keen eyes' grace, which she irradiates
upon the woman of this female divinity
        who cradles her now,
        sweeping her in an invisible clasp as she floats, braced by finger-
             holds, footholds in small clefts,
                rock-grooves, dents,
        dangerously passing across the wide midriff to a new markswoman-
snapshooter's vantage, in command of
        her divine model,
        artist capturing in her miniaturizing box's magic color frames
             exact wallet-size likenesses,
                twins of a grand
        oriental giantess, China-doll deity. . . . I, voyeur and adorer of you
both,
spring and cavort on my cliff-top
        balcony, the toy
        of my body—doll to myself—bursting alive with a strange new joy,
             no more a foreigner in this place,
                I am strung out
and coming unstrung in my bones, swinging loose from the bonds
of shoulder-pegs and hip-pins, jolly
        in marionette-strings
        of tendons, ligaments. Oh, from birth the buried doll-Buddha life
             of our body wills this release.
                Japanese satoris
of the pores. Each hair's root wakes, each hair freed in dance!

THE KOFUKUJI ARSONISTS

In Kofukuji museum stands a phalanx
of august statues—stone, clay and bronze figures—
salvaged from two millennia of lordly
firebugs (can Japanese pyromania,
a dominant trait, be carried in the genes?). . . .

From era to era, embattled warlords
sped to be first to set fire to shrine or sacred
temple, each breathless to outpace the rival.
At midnight, all the sculpted deities, gathered
withindoors, relive their heroic couplings
to long-dead hermit priests who rescued them
throughout history, the monks keeping one jump
ahead of the royal incendiaries—
those feuding clans! Conflagrations erupt
like brushfires on a sun-baked hillside, each sparked

by insult or stain of honor. Yet always,
century after century, the exile
monk, life-taken-between-the-teeth outlaw
from both factions, steals into the blaze, leaps
through the circle of flames, and flying, wingless,

through the collapsing doorway, dodges falling
rafter, crumbling doorjamb—each a hoop of fire:
he must race flame-tongues licking across the walls,
sweeping interior chambers. A Kofukuji
student monk, trained in soldiership, always saves,
first, Kannon Bosatsu (the thousand-handed,
eleven-faced squatting Goddess of Mercy):
hoisting the statue, braced on the fireman's
carry-hold of his crossed forearms, or hefted
up high on his back; and then, tumbling backwards

through the flaming rubble, he drops to one knee,
perhaps, to dash out the sparks and swat away
white-hot embers that threaten to scorch her outer
skin—a shell of gold leaves, in a few spots the kiln-baked
gilt layer charring through, nearly exposing

the tougher second skin of japanned lacquer—
a hard black gloss of laminated varnish

miraculously resisting hottest coals,
the many-layered shellac epidermis
warding off demonic forked snake-tongues of flame . . .
He ignores the sizzling mouths of fire, open-
throated, gaping widely over his back
and flanks, soundless wails through the wounds of maws
in his scratchy haircloth shirt. He does not see
her thousand arms grow limber and soft, the frantic

waving of her hands brushing firebrands away
from all sides of his body as he flees: a few
dozen hands cupped and smothering the charred lips
of holes in his cloak; a few hands whisking the flamelets
(fingers of fire) away from his face and bare skull;

others, caressing and sheltering his singed—
but unfired—beard. Each of her eleven faces,
springing to life with a different expression,
assumes a guise to fortify his nerve
or ease his pain. He communes with the many-visaged
deity, taking strength from her glances—
smiles, grimaces, scowls, radiant beckonings . . .
He laughs outright, boldly gives thanks; then chides
his innocence, curses her for a Gorgon
in disguise—Medusa! He shuts his eyes, hurtles

through the smoldering egress, life, limb and saved
Goddess intact, barrelling from the ash-heap
ruins . . . Sequestered in the outlying forest,
his laughter returns in a great timber-
splintering roar, irrepressible. . . .

IN PURSUIT OF THE ANGEL
(for Frederick Morgan)

I. WING PLUMES OF THE THIEF

Late afternoon. One hour before sunset. The water level
—sinking slowly away—
exposes the crowns of barely submerged
coral heads, altering the unbroken flat plain of offshore shoals

to a museum of pinnacles and arches,
alternately bulbous and square-skulled statuary
jutting into the bay,
solid replicas of the few cumulus thunderheads spoiling the pool-
pure azure of fair skies. . . . I mount
the upreared convolutions of brain coral, amazed at my sudden
heaviness, as, stooping,
I creep on gloved palms and flippers, wary
of scraping knee or elbow (the merest scratch is a wound!)—
then using my speargun as cane,
I hobble upright on a flat center promontory
stretching tall, tall,
taller—for all my knock-kneed wobbliness—than any mammalian
biped, and wave my arms, squawking

to my snorkeler-buddy, face-down, gliding between two star
coral reefs, oblivious
(in another galaxy) to the instant sculptures
jewel-studding the surface, as he weaves a zigzag path, foraging

for shellfish—lobsters, crabs,
molluscs—in hollows of the coral. From vantage
of my aerial perch,
he grapples between the furrowed gap-toothed jaws of an alligator,
the great notched maw is closing,
but the corrugated fish pail afloat in the inflated truck inner tube
wedges those gums
open and breaks the bite, tugging the nylon
drawcord tied to his weight belt. He spins around to check out
the snag, grins at the clown
poised on one leg, arms spreadeagled, sashaying
like a model: together,

we behold the arrested aviary! The hundreds of birds, circling
and diving all day—bunched over

crisscrossing and interlaced schools of mackerel, gar, jack
and kingfish moiling
in the choppy waters just beyond the surf—
have come to roost, poised on the coral shelves: the pelicans

float on their feather-cushioned
haunches, comatose; the gulls and frigate birds,
slightly bowed over,
wings folded, stand in obeisance to spreadwinged erect cormorants,
black-bottomed muscular swimmers
that chase underwater prey: now, in peacock-spanned grandeur,
they extend waterlogged
plumes to dry in the sun. . . . My reign ended,
I drop to a squat. The nearest shag leans forward, dips
—wings outstretched, unmoving—
approaches a belly-flop, then flaps both wings, heavily
dragging its tail
in the water, and snatches a half-alive plump queen triggerfish
from our exposed bucket! Kicking

and splashing with his wide flat feet, a running takeoff,
he ascends. I jump,
rubber webbed-feet first, into the shallows,
replacing the canvas cover . . . *I rescue the fallen wing plume.*

II. IN PURSUIT OF THE ANGEL

The horizon's wide ax-blade cleaves the sun's disc: poised hemisphere
of fire, hung aloft, floats
for an unearthly long moment, windless,
as if choosing between sea and sky, shrinks to less,
less—a least flare dwindles, dies. *It is a pureness
of vanishing* . . . The constant five
or six rows of surf, alternately humped wave-
backs and foamy breakers, have shifted
from inshore shallows
to the bay's perimeter, as if flowing wrinkles of sea
surface carpet were smoothed

to the far end of the rug. Now belly-floating, just beyond
                    the sand bar, indolent, I
idle in thirty-foot-deep clear water.
    Iridescent glitter on sea-floor shells looms near,
    detail of bottom flora as starkly visible
        as my hand's magnified knuckles.
            Everything in view seems within arm's reach,
            but fish grow scarce in this calm
                transparency,
                and squatter birds are thinning out, casting about dreamily
                    toward the roiling food-chain

cycle waters of the bay-mouth . . . Memory. *I backstroke six hours*
                    in my mind's eye rerun.
See again the direct stark light of midday,
    blinding at high noon. Sunny or overcast, the glare
    on live and dead particles—minutiae—thickens
        to an opaque wall of murkiness,
            impenetrable as dense fog. I feel
            suspended in liquid cotton.
                Partial clear-ups
                are worse. The bottom looms close, sways out far. All surfaces
                tilt, weave from side to side.

Objects teeter, warp—they lose and get back their shapes. I must
                    squint, or shut my eyes, often
to stop the vertigo and nausea.
    But now, in this twilight saliency, eyes touch
    like fingertips: sight extends the body, stretched
        nerves threading the water—seeingness
            grows its own skin, sensitive, sensitive!
            I drop slowly from the surface,
                letting reverse
                gravity and my free fall momentum balance, reaching
                a stillstand, for moments,

then slipping down some inches. Halfway to the bottom, I drift,
                    musing, past a bouquet
of anemones, their many tentacles
    waving slowly. I touch one petal-shaped tuber,
    and the whole colony of blooms shrinks into tight buds—
        my eye recoils, a stunned flower

itself, puzzled at the vanishing blossom
quantities of atomized
   anemone. I
   stare and stare. They do not reinflate! . . . *If all distances*
     seem close up, what happens

to up close? I force my eyes to focus nearer, the effort
         to adjust my irises
like switching binoculars from mountain
   skyline to shoelaces and blond leg-hairs. Scanning
   minutely down lengths of my forearm and spear
     gun, my dilating pupils clamp
      a few cubic milliliters of plankton,
     scrutinizing the carnival
       gala. Minuscule
       acrobatics whirl in refracted light, the tiny lives
        spinning upon themselves—

dazzle to dim, sparkle to fade—dancing and effervescing,
         luminous as fireflies. . . .
Near bottom in the shallow inshore basin,
   I'm lured by rainbow-flash of a queen angelfish
   and swim toward the drop-off beyond the outer coral
    reefs, settling downward. I descend
      along a slope, cruising parallel to sand
      bar's steep gradient. Diving fast
       with my back and hips—
        flippers undulating, hardly moving a limb, I circle
        the fish for visual feast,

nearly colliding with a wide high-backed flat sheet of tin.
         It turns to face my advance.
The sudden narrowness of body,
   in front view, magnifies the bulbous eyes—a spadefish!
   Nearly circular, it measures perhaps three feet
    in diameter, more a shield
     or skillet than a shovelhead: so wide
     and gleaming in profile, queerly
      tubular head-on.
       It swims, by a succession of nervous rushes, and hair-
        trigger turns. Soon, it is met

by a fleet of thirty or forty spadefish, mostly small fry,
                swimming in formation:
largest members, near the front and middle
    of the ranks; the smallest, around the periphery,
    a few not able to keep up with the school.
        Broadside on, they wrest my full
            horizontal compass of vision—I must
            rotate my neck from side to side
                to take them all in.
                If I release a shot at them, wildly, how can I miss
                    hitting two at a time?

I try to single out a large target, but I lose tracery
                of separate outlines.
They overlap so much, I can see no gaps
    between them: a mosaic—continuous—
    of interlocking tin fish-shapes. As I fumble,
        taking aim, a stout front steersman
            pivots into reverse, and the whole colony
        turns with him, swivelling, folded
            upon each other—
                though none touch! *A shuffler's trick with a deck of cards.*
                Halfway into the turn, all

catch the light at once and emit a single blinding flash!
                Now in the rear, the helms-
man chases the group. He pivots again.
    Bizarrely, the others follow his rearguard lead.
    Still puzzling over the odd chain of command,
        I, accidentally, fire a spear.
            A frenzied blur. Fish are scattered, hurtling,
            in all directions at once. Spot-
                light bursts! I blink,
                again and again . . . *As swiftly, the dozens of loose cards*
                fly back into the deck.

III. THE BLACK HOLES

The school of vexed spadefish sweeps in a parabolic downward
                curve—luminescent blade
of a great scythe cutting a wide deep sea
    swathe—and drops out of sight. *Swift evacuation!*
    I am left with so much just-emptied space, a hollow
        waiting to be filled. What is holding

its watery breath? It seems that I'm surrounded
by a great collapsed lung, dreaming
   the next inhalation.
   Can the vast sea choke on its own deflatedness, drowning
      in a short-winded void?

Bubbles, bubbles rising! Detritus falling, filling the black
                              holes, a constant thick rain
of live and dead matter to lightless depths.
   My eye zeroes in on minute diatoms: tissue-bits,
   thin beings—slender threads of life raining down
      from the surface, never to touch
         bottom! The many frail sliver-lives, cut short
         in midfall, are food for bottom
            feeders . . . *Oh, constant*
            gift of nutriment falling from genial skies of upper sea!
               Nothing starves! Nothing starves!

FLAMINGOS OF THE SODA LAKES

They are standing, or stalking, in clouds—
                clouds of steam
welling up from the earth, vapors
        endlessly rising and fading to a thin mist:
                their bodies
        are pink-white balls of smoke,
                        clouds themselves,
ghostly feathered-eggs of solid
        cloud bobbing gently on jointed stilts,
                apparitional,
        great flocks of heavy smoke-ovals
                        suspended in the upward-
thinning mists of smoke-haze. . . .
        Thousands are waiting their turn to drink,
                thousands
        squeezed into the tight circles
                        surrounding thermal hot
springs studding Lake Hannington's shores,
                overflowing, and slowly draining into the lake;
                thousands
        athirst and athirst, waiting
                        to drop their long
snaking necks to the water to drink.
        The heads—flowers too heavy for their stems—
                loll
nervously over the always horizontal
                        body-ovals. Now
the necks—those willowy S's—
        reversing their curves, swing the heads in a great
                semicircle
        with a cranklike swivelling
                        down to the boiling
shallows where they float, weightless,
        bobbing like buoys; and they swill great drafts
                of fuming earth-
        water through the leathery-soft petals
                        of their inverted bills.
As they drink they dance, they long-
        leggedly skip and trot, leaping in steambaths,
                a splendid
        prancing on their arrowy stiff limbs,

hopping up and down,
teetering, shifting their top-heavy
    weight lopsidedly from leg to leg-pole, never losing
    their balance;
  their necks undulating slowly, rhythmically,
      adjusting the spoons
of their half-submerged upside-down bills
    as they guzzle the boiling waters, keeping time
    with their legs'
  waltzing gait a-waggle from side to side,
      while they shudder in exquisite
pain: whether more from the quaffed hot
    rivers siphoning up their long necks and scalding
    their throats,
  or more from the fierce hot foamy effervescence
      of the wading pools
that scorch their frail lower legs. . . .
    Now many are ruffling wingquills and little nubs
    of tail-feathers,
  warning rivals to make way and stand clear,
      jealously guarding
their small dunking-and-dipping tracts;
    and a few are butting each other with their flanks
    and tufted rears,
  jockeying closer and closer to the wellsprings,
      where the fresh mineral
overflow waters from underground streams
    seep up through the lakeshore mud; closer to the pure
    clear waters
  of health, earth-filtered and effervescing,
      where the hissing sub-
terranean gases meet the clean open air,
    mixing their purities, cleansing over and over:
    refinings:
earth   air   water   light: where the sizzling
      earth-waters flow
into the fetid, brackish soda of the dense
    alkaline lake which, imbibed in large drafts, is noxious
    like seawater—
soda and salt, breeders of multitudes
      of unicellular life-
motes, poisons to higher forms: life-givers,
    life-takers.

Flamingos, gladly suffering throat-burns
leg-burns,
suffering infernal hots for the pure, dance
away the agonies
of hellfires for earth's life-elixirs,
dancing for flames of wet that cannot singe a feather,
dancing
to fill with firewater to satiety,
to fill with flames
that cannot sear the long white angel
plumes of their wings: a dancing to satiety—
satieties
of thirstfire—a thirst dance!

BLUE HERON

At the lowest tides, in mudflat shallows,
you stall at the edge, and wait;
or try wading, a few inches deep, with strides
so leisurely and trancing
your slender jointed stilts are reeds, lolling
                    indolently,
their sway merging with the laziest interlacings
          of invisible shore currents.

The air's pulse slows,
learns *caress*,
the soft frictions of encirclement.

Small winds, brushing your neck-feathers, slacken,
coax a few fine cilia to wave;
the slowest breathing riffles the hair
of feathers—endures the lofty poise of another's chill.

A self on stilts, your long lines
are a triumph of refusals:
no feeder more quiet, none more elegant and poised.
You fish the low tide, fastidious, aristocratic.
Altitude is a keenness of eye, a stare
               that trains the long light
to compact its blooms into vertical sightings.

Poise chastens the arrogance of horizontal beaks.
Erectness lengthens the slender poles of being.

II. Wreckage of the Pagoda Moons

MACAW AND PARAKEET
(for Dave Smith)

We take turns keeping
the two birds
perched on our shoulders.
The girls squeal
when the macaw

nips their cheeks
or earlobes. The parakeet
loves human saliva
mixed in its food,
says Mrs. Tamura. The small

bird cupped in her hands
pecks saliva-mixed
birdseed from the tip
of her tongue,
flicking

in and out. She teaches
the children
to feed her long-tailed
darling with pointy tongues. . . .
Isaac falls

into trance, the macaw
on his clavicle:
reading horror comics,
he demands
the sliding shoji-doors

be kept shut
behind him. He slips
deeper and deeper into the bird's
hypnotic jabbering.
She pricks his ear, cheek,

neck—harder and faster.
Shrewd despot!
He winces in pain,
but her squawks
hold him entranced, absently

puzzled (as he reads)
by his odd tolerance
of the macaw's
exquisite torture. He seals
himself off

from other humans, accepts
more and more
discomfort: grumbles,
twitches, quarrels,
groans. . . .

INTERVIEW

(Lake Shinobazu, Ueno Park, Tokyo)

I.

Lady,
how long you been driving a bus?
No long.
The bus rides me.
Drive, lady, not ride.
And why prefer you the night shifts?
Night? Who rides nights?
It's morning!

II.

We glide the sleek abandoned streets
face-high into morning,
snatch the roving sun from secret poise each dawn,
and plaster the fleeting gold on the windshield glass
like a fine shiny paste.
But don't it get lonely, lady, all night? So quiet is alone.
And lovely the quiet.
Who lacks company, when drunk?
A bus is roomy and the air fresh as ponds.
Each bend round the lake-edge enlivens.
A storm, now and then, is good for surprises.
But the calm jaunts are cleaner. And when it's clear
the views are so brittle and crisp
I wince each time I stare.
So close to the panes,
nestled erect and propped in the plummetting flat half-face
(a prodigious forehead,
no jaw to absorb the sensuous punch of the weather),
I traffic in close-ups
and feast on the graphs of my eyes.

III.

But lady,
what do you do for noise?
Such voices, those cries.
I wade ear-deep in a sky-full of birds.

NARA PARK: TWILIGHT DEER FEEDING

Toward evening, sky's aqua
darkens to ultramarine,
strangely brighter over bald Mount Wakakusa
(treeless, dry grasses burnt in annual
January fete) than over wooded Mount Kasuga,
abode of the gods. . . . We reenter these grounds—temple of the pagodas—
hurrying before sundown, before nightfall and the closing of gates,
bearing handfuls of small crackers
to offer the genial deer

one last, shy, long-nosed feeding.
We stroll in the deserted park,
dawdling. Are we sneak thieves? Or benefactors?
Why do we meander and leer behind?
It is twilight limbo. The deer, orbiting fitfully
in pairs all afternoon, now slink in passels of ten or twelve, or lurk
in shaded hedgerows. At our approach, they seem to dance sideways.
Or they float in sleep-languor,
neither toward nor away

from our glum coos and purrings
(now it is we who beg, not fawns
or does) . . . They move in weightless stupor,
a graceful bouncing on soft footpads
of paws, their just-lighter-than-air hindquarters
pitched to and fro, as if earth were sponge-turf on springs—flocks
of wingless, thin seraphim gliding across grassy cloud
scud, green cloudbanks of sod.
The children sidle up

to a lone deer—strayed a few feet
from its group; he backs away,
sweeping with a band of others to semi-seclusion
in a glen of cedars. No hideaway . . . The after-
glow of long-spent sunset, a pinkish tint on lawns
fading to lemon-sallow glimmerings, pastes a faint layer of luminous
glaze, momentarily, on all surfaces—embrace of the last light.
Halos of muted light, in enchanted
low-toned brilliance,

encircle tree rinds, deer hides,
shrines. Temple walls shimmer.
The sheen floods near and recedes in flashes,
light recoiling upon the beholder's eyes,
hypnotic—we blink, to no effect. The unearthly glow
dims, slowly fades into degrees of gray, the pinkish second skin
falling away, sliding off each surface. . . . A cycle of toots,
high-pitched, eerie, pierces
the blanketing dusk!

Horn-blasts from an unseen trumpeter.
Scores of deer leap in unison,
springing from many quarters, well over a hundred
becoming visible at once. Emerging from the woods
in a full three-hundred-sixty-degree circle around us,
as if born spontaneously from the horn which summons them (a punctual
daily signal), they converge upon a wisteria grove for sanctuary.
Following their course, the girls
try to intercept two

frail stragglers, arms outstretched
to enwrap each creature.
But the wiry featherweights, undeflected, with no
visible change in speed or direction,
slip past the puzzled children shaking their heads.
One fawn appears to pass, miragelike, through my stooping son's
hips and shoulder—in my sideview, a figure crosshatched,
composed of shimmering diamonds
and spheroids of light;

in frontview, scrawnier and leggy,
slim as an angelfish
encountered, face to face, through underwater
mask. The keeper, bugler of moments
before, appears, waving a short flexible switch;
feebly snapping the whip, he herds some two-hundred-odd deer
into deep low pens. . . . Instantaneously, scattered dots
of light, mirrored on the surface
of Sarusawa Pond,

brighten! Whirling about-face, we witness
a spectacle of colorful lanterns:
well-lit octagonals and hexagonals, distributed

everywhere in view, within or without
the park. Of those nearest to us, half are stone lanterns
fastened to shrine walls, benches, or trelliswork. The other half, hung
aloft, metal lanterns suspended from roof eaves or oak limbs,
sway gently in the breeze—rainbow
phantasmagoria overhead!

WRECKAGE OF THE PAGODA MOONS
(Kofukuji Temple, Nara)

Nothing moves
or murmurs but ourselves, as light
fails and fails—
all but an eerie shimmer
that comes and goes on shrine-walls and gravel path-
ways. Dusk thickens. Pools
and patches of shade merge in shadow—
unbroken dimness,
tans of oaken and cedar walls
deepening to sepias . . .
We circle the temple grounds, struck by absence, hush

of evacuation—
no stampede of gawky tourists
or prattle of guides.
Light winds enfold the deer park's
thousand wooded acres, relics and sacred pavilions
in quiescent chill, wrapping
the exquisite pagoda upper stories, square-
balconied, in mist . . .
Carla, thieving a last glimpse
of the turtle pond
behind her, bawls surprise. We all halt, turnabout.

A horizontal tower
stretches, in flattened repose,
to a recumbent length
double the height of its model,
or vertical too-solid twin: the five-storied pagoda
casting a long silhouette,
finely detailed black borders pasted
on starker white;
the midday showcase transformed
from a tub for scores
of tortoises, inching up and down the bank, to whitewash!

A moon-lit sheet
of fire . . . Hovering on the pool-edge,
we can see both
the iridescent sparkle of light
playing over shallow bottom-rocks and mirrored details
in the swan's-neck-sloping eaves
of the pagoda's profile. The moon, floating
beside the third level
tier, lights the balconies
of the near side etching
a lacy filigree, leaving the intricate far side roofs

eerily darkened. . . .
Stunned, we turn from the standing
to the sleeping tower
and back, comparing. *No signals.*
By a shared impulse, unspoken, two daughters and father
bend for skipping stones to hurl,
and soon we are flinging one missile after another
at the towering monument
of shadow, our throws altering
from lateral tosses—
sidearm casts to induce flippity-flops over the surface—

to two-handed heaves
of larger rocks and boulders,
the playful glint
in our eyes varying to warriors'
glower: hurl by hurl, we work off our spleen
and funk born of the months
of difficult awe before all monuments, ceremony.
How much power we wield!
Power to shatter into splintering
fragments of light
the perfected ikon of centuries. And power to dismantle

the moon's two-fold
replicas, the gleaming silver disc
pasted on the water's
dimmed creamy glaze. *Both moons.*
The twenty-one-carat-silver luminescent wafer.
The glistening tin alloy
overspreading the surface. *Both moons—mirror
and worn medallion—
fractured into shadow-light slivers
blended with the pagoda's
saw-edged chunks into the one blazing swirl of wreckage.*

YOSHINO: FALSE DAWN OF THE CHERRY BLOSSOM

The town hugs the crest of a ridge which ascends, steeply,
to the hill summit.
The one paved road skirts
four mammoth cherry-
tree groves, amassed at graduated levels,
each uphill wood peaking
into full blossom a week or two later in the season
than its downhill cousin. . . . We arrive
in wrong heavy rains,
greeted by untrimmed shrubs,
unscheduled

ruts in the road, soft tar-patches fixing too slowly.
We are *off season.*
Boxed-in in the tramway's slow
squat cable car,
we are wafted up the cliff's sweeping incline,
children leaping from side to side,
front to rear. The rickety tram-cab, quaking stiffly,
shrieks on its ungreased cables.
We disembark midway
up Yoshino Mountain, mecca
of the cherry

blossoms. We pass acres of wilted lavender plum blossoms,
their late-winter prime
a month past, followed by thousands
of cherry trees—
all branches and stems as densely laden
with swelled buds as comb-cells
in hives choked with honey. Weeks early, what a splurge
of pinkish-white snows of bloom
we miss! Oh how
can we come and go, oblivious
to blossom

harvest, implores our guide, who is sorry she cannot
hurry the cherry trees,
cannot coax the stalled cherry buds
to bloom faster.

She would try and try, but she cannot speed up
the slow-rising sap that dreams
its way, lazily, up from roots through needles of stems
into buds. There is no way to bypass
the ancient slow
circulatory systems of thousand-
year-old trunks,

numb sleepers in a world heartland of flowering forests.
No, *we* are to blame.
We are sorry to be untimely,
sorry to miss
the burgeoning glory, the cyclone-gush of blooms.
But we can love slow trees,
those sleeping bronze uncles—we will savor the dumb sleep
of buds, the dozing curled petals. . . .
I hunt for glimmers
of love in sprigs of just-missed cherry
blossom laced

in your hair, unbloomed, heavily budded all the same,
a sprig in my lapel,
a sprig in the lovely cleft
between your ear
and scalp, another in the ornamental vase
on the table—none ever to flower!
Gladly, I'll keep these too-green hastily plucked switches
of miscarried cherry lives: the beaded
necklaces, pony-tail-ties,
bracelets and anklets encircling our blue-
veined limbs!

THE HUMAN BOMB
(for Dave Smith)

Trained
to fit himself delicately
under the frame of a U.S. tank,
and blow himself up—
this man,
the only failed survivor
of his batallion, recounts to me how
for months each day he practiced
and refined the art
of detonating
the near-invisible
humpbacked or potbellied bomb
of the self: daily
cleansing
from the skullbox womb
all thought, purging all feeling
and impulse but the singleminded mindless
will to empty and to fill
with Glory,
Glory, greater Glory
to the Emperor Immortal: the head
a scoured-clean shell
alchemizing
into a powder-keg, the mind
a taut fuse—suppose an erect
phallus between the eyes!—the spirit
a matchstick, its one allowed
move
a single flick
to ignite the fuse's combustible
tip: this wry, limber
pintsized
Oriental, pushing fifty,
math professor at Nagoya Uni-
versity telling me how, just last week,
unhelmeted and empty-handed,
he leapt
into a homicidal wrangle
between student radicals and resister-
moderates (now in slapstick

pantomime
acting out for us
his bold leaps of intervention):
and how, strangely, both disputants
bowed in dignified
full
doubled-over waistbend
obeisance to his naked bald pate:
who, taking his daily
mortal
unflinching campus
life-risks for peace, is distressed
beyond remedy by his ten-year-old
son's accusations
of coward-
liness. . . . The soft life.

LOCKJAW

I. YOKO TO HONO

All jutting-out jaw,
no teeth, more English than you let on—
longshoreman unloading and packaging
my hold baggage, you say this huge used crate
will do for the job—*good box, good box!*
Yes, yes. But will it hold up, dollied from hull
to boxcar REA Express, halfway
around the world? *So, so. Aso desu.*

You reach inside,
finding a ripped-open forgotten
small carton of books—all the same, all new,
fresh from the publisher—and hand me
a copy. *Presento. Special Service.*
A book of magic and the occult,
amateurish and low-brow, published
by obscure Oakland-Cal. firm, upgraded

by Tokyo outfit.
My lucky find. . . .
                    Aoki zips by
on his motorbike, rules stevedores
from customs end to end on old-style
thick-tired pedal bikes. The men packing
my crate delicately fold and wrap
the Nipponese blankets and futon mats,
then slap my wife's choice ceramic pots

into misshapen
great wads of newspaper. And the kids'
stilts, which she insisted we pack—now
I'm not sure this one massive ramshackle
crate wasn't picked to accommodate
the stilts, which one man places on top,
diagonally. A tight squeeze, but . . .
it all fits—his smirk offers the stilts

as final proof: all
choices were right. How lucky we are.
So cheap a job, so good a box . . .
                                    Customs.

The inspector punches out stickers
from a rapid-fire motorized handgun,
hitting all my valises and satchels,
extra stickers flying everywhichway.
I pass through the turnstile. He interposes

a blind, bland grin.
(*Take home all the goodies you please, Gaijin.*)

II. HONO TO FRISCO

Jolted down the service
elevator, an open three-sided cage
(skeleton of steel, its tiers of black cross-
bones creaking in descent), I spring awake,
teetering back on my worn-through sneakers' soles
in a vast warehouse, many lackadaisacal
workers milling about, idly lounging:
all native dock hands—officials

and underlings alike—
dressed in flouncy shirts with gaudy rainbow
prints: loose-sleeved, pleated, baggy. The free-
lancer, freeloader, softsell wheeler
dealer expression painted on all
the faces . . .
                No hydraulic lift
to lower the box, it, too, is taxied
by rickety elevator, drops

too fast! My seventeen-
hundred-fifty pound secondhand crate,
sturdy and iron-hinged, looms before me:
two or three boards cracked and gaping, metal
joints all down one edge snapped through, the seal
yet intact . . .
                I'm greeted by no-nonsense
baggage checker, thin-lipped, cool, smiling:
the crate must be opened, every nook

inspected. Baggage
Master to my left. Customs Master
to my right. Both counselling decision.
Neither offering advice. I must

register the box, in bond, to be cleared
through Chicago customs (at untold
dear expense). Or I must hire a couple
of idle dock thugs to pry the box

    open with crowbars,
then supervise the reassemblage
in time to get the knotty shambles lugged
back into the hold this afternoon,
despatching it UNACCOMPANIED
to San Francisco . . .
             Tongue-tied, I pay two
of the loose-jointed idlers twenty
dollars apiece to proceed with open-chest

    surgery. They motion
to snap the hoops of steel banding
that encircle the whole frame to shorten
the work. I resist, more and more
feebly—the bands are severed, whipping out
and away:
          I see black coils of straggled
celluloid wildly spilling from reels
of a jammed movie projector . . . now lithe

    and sinewy flat snakes . . .
now shimmery metal tape rulers, unwound
suddenly, snapping and vibrating
this way and that . . .
          I feel the nausea
starting. My body shudders, recoils
at the waste of binding strength, those steely
girths lost forever, my corpus needing
its own tough ligaments and tendons—

    irreplaceable
connective tissues! I come to my senses,
my skinalarms . . .
          The men begin
jimmying open one corner of the crate,
nails flying one way, wood-chips and long
icicle-splinters another   I
am screaming   *Halt*   *Oh stop, stop*   *Nail it*
back   *Nail it back, before it's too late*

     in a fury to reverse
time, to make the last five minutes run
backward on the clock . . .
                        Now they're pounding
the uncoiled black snakes back on the box
with three-inch nails. The more serious worker,
older and taller of the two, drives
each nail partway into the box—
½ inch perhaps—then knocks the nail-

     head sideways. The shorter
man whacks all the nails up to the hilt,
burying a few nailtops in the boards
totally, indiscriminate
of the box's fragile contents . . .
                     My head
in such a whirl as to yes or no,
I can only glower and stammer
and—voiceless—curse my regrets. *My lockjaw.*

RIDING THE DUFFLE

This crazy overstuffed khaki duffle
with raincoats and galoshes bulging out the top
wriggles and flops and gyrates on my back like a netted crocodile.
Jackknifed, doubling up
to keep the drooping sack-bottom aloft,
I shamble and lurch in crude dance-step, shuffle
to the tune of

"Daddy, shame on you. You're scrunched down
and humpbacked like an old beggar man."
Smoothening my long spine's accordion from neck
to waist, I unflex erect,

hoist the stiff-cotton denim barrel
of two or three changes of thermal long underdrawers
for five, giving it one great bounce,
bucking with my hip and coccyx
and the arch at the small of my back: the burden lands squarely—
in a sort of floppy deadman's carry—
on my upright shoulder:

I spruce up to look Sapporo Olympian—
giraffine at thirty-seven—
to the sage accusing Methuselah eyes of twelve. . . .
Somehow we pass through the narrow wicket

gate where the uniformed attendant,
squatting in a little shallow box-seat with his kerosene-oil
heater between his legs—eerily aglow—
punches tickets between grunts.
Hordes of commuters swarming past,
he always finds time to grin at my blond son, to punch
a few imaginary holes

in his fingertips and earlobes,
and mutter a phrase or two of near-English
endearingly to him. We climb
the long flights of stairs to the train

platform as if paddling upstream, or torpedoed
by the rough currents
of cramming and jostling kimono-clad

lady octogenarians.
Safely aboard the limited express to Tokyo station—
our first bout with the commuter anthill
squeeze of crush-hour traffic—the kids bolt down the aisle

to scramble for seats. None left! Fighting the side-to-side
twist and torsion of the car's
bucking and quaking as it accelerates to full speed
in a few seconds, pitching from my heels

to cowboy-boot toes, no leeway
to reach for the short loops of leather ceiling straps
and get my balance, I hurry
to pile all the larger handbags and satchels
in one temporary midcar loading zone;
now helping the girls to lift umbrellas, ponchos and parkas,
overstuffed schoolbags (acres

of homework on a three-day outing to Kyoto?)
to the overhead narrow
shelves; now coaxing my son
to evacuate the suicidal sliding-door entrance-

way quick before the next stop: *Kawasaki, gozaimus. Kawasaki,*
blares the matronly voice over the mike, I
lurch sidewise to rescue
the floor-luggage too late, a close
swipe, my hand just grazing the handle of my black valise
(those precious manuscripts!), missing by a hair's
breadth. Whump. Heave ho,

I'm lifted and hurled across the cabin by three rows
of barrelling narrow columns of flesh,
each line-up of bodies bulldozed
from behind by a thickset

stocky "pusher" with a retired sumo wrestler's physique
jamming an overflow surplus
of too-willing martyrs—human sausages—
through the gate. Somehow I get three fingers twined round the long
dufflebag belt and chain
hauling the lumpy bulk after me for anchorage—
sandbagging, as in a hurricane!

I come to a safe landing, absurdly
seated on the turned-upright duffle blasted
into the railingbars beside the doorway
glutted with heads and limbs. Two satchels have vanished.

Bobbing atop the denim bellbuoy,
I search. In the lull between station squalls,
peering through dust-haze,
I spot a small coat on the floor and hallucinate
my son's mangled thin-boned toy
carcass underfoot.
In terror, I bawl each child's two-syllabled name. When I pause

for breath, I hear a volley
of familiar squeals and chuckles. I spot all three
kids installed at the far end
of the car in two opposite half-seats, cater-cornered,

squeezed beside dozing slim dowager suburbanites.
Swaying on my lighthouse
watchtower,
I get a clear view of the whole railways'
crammed unsinkable vessel.
An all-seeing—if powerless—navigator,
I survey the whirlpool

herd of milling and eddying black heads, my girls
in their cramped quarters
folding and shaping delicate little origami flowers—
a hiccuping farmhand in baggy overalls

presides over them with hand-signals,
half-falling in the nearer child's lap at each bounce
of the heaving train. Ah! I know that wince
of hers—she scowls less
from bumps and jolts than from fumes of exhaled sake
she gladly suffers to add to her rapidly growing repertory
of origami characters.

Oh how she'd deplore her daddy, tipsy:
"Stop the air pollution. You'll asphyxiate us."
In a side-aisle seat, alongside,
I espy her mother's pepper-and-salt short bob dropped

floorward, who shuffles,
fishing out of her basket-weave straw-mesh purse
two slender long implements—
not chopsticks, surely?—oh, brushes,
and bottles of sumie paints.
Her sketchpad fallen open in her lap, she glances
up and down,

blinks at an oddly displaced
pair of long legs arched and hugging a potato-shaped
bag—a wobbly stool and wardrobe—and lifts her eyes
to her bemused spouse: guffaws

once, loudly and uncontrollably, as I pass
my hand over my skull
bumps unable to locate the cap of a dunce
she drafts with a few quick strokes of her brush, then hunts
for a more inspiring model.
Yokohama, rumbles the P.A. mike, low-
toned, embellished with three styles of sorry and thank you,

begging your pardon, please.
I brace myself for a tidal wave of pounding legs
and trunks, fumbling in my pocket Berlitz
for imprecations to hurl at the sea of oblivious faces

all about me, hoping to wheedle a few dutiful citizen-recruits
to dive for my lost two black samsonite
bags, when both bag-grips
are eased into my hand at once, the retrievers'
hands withdrawn so deftly
I cannot identify
the right two pairs of eyes

to thank. We come to a groaning halt.
The doors swing wide. I suck in my chest.
We pause at the scrimmage
between incoming and outgoing floods: the intercontinental

divide at midsea where heavy crosscurrents, matched,
cancel each other out:
a ghostly stasis
from the balance of mighty opposing forces.
Pockets of dank hot air, stalled pools,
hold momentary truce with the few light billows
of cool incoming station breezes:

the deceptive surface-calm of the undertow
before a huge wave crests.
The disembarking mob files out in two orderly rows
to right and left

circumnavigating the impenetrable polite
front-line battalion,
waiting for the signal to break ranks. Then,
the thunder of galloping boot-heels seems to precede
by a scant margin
forked lightning of plunging heads and grotesque pained faces,
neck-veins swelling like hoses,

glaring eyes. The floorboards buckle.
The whole car shimmies like a tent in a gale.
A few unfortunates are flung against
the locked-shut double doors opposite the entrance.

They squirm and flail, their cheeks,
forearms and leg-shanks
plastered against the glass—protozoans
squiggling between glass sheets of microscope slides—
so flattened their knobs of bones
seem to collapse in skin-bags, deflating hides.
One stout man, wedged

into the handrail, makes a valiant thrust
to escape. He's frozen, pinned to the horizontal bars.
He turns to make his puffed backside
cushion the tonnage of bodies glued together by torque-whip force

as the train rounds a bend, the cars lurching.
Do his eyes accept, ungrudgingly,
anonymous body fusing, as creases in his palms take grime,
his lungs invisible Tokyo air-silts and scums?
Next stop, an obscure hamlet.
A man enters in soiled workclothes, tape measure in one hand,
three-legged footstool in the other, blunt

pencil behind one ear. He speedily elbows
his way through the sardine-
packed crowd, hops on his stool, leafs several colorful posters
lovingly, one by one,

from a thick stack
tucked under his shirt, and, with two lightning swift
flicks of his wrist,
removes last week's obsolete cancelled ads
from their picture frame casements, replacing them with glossy
shining color-plate novelties,
many displaying garish half-veiled sexual poses.

This man, a hop-trotting gnome, unstoppable
as he sidestrokes, breaststrokes,
dog-paddles across throngs to get from wall to wall:
I saw him, face-down, do a deadman's float—

in a dream, was it?—
over the serried unbroken ranks of shoulder-bones
and skulls pressed close:
he glided so delicately across those body tenements,
scalp-and-clavicle shingles
of human roofing, no one seemed
to notice, or mind.

He might have been a butter-
fly or hummingbird weightlessly flapping
his lighter-than-air
wings up there on his commercial pollinating

rounds, sailing unnoticed alike
over conductor and peripatetic ticket-taker,
and gently flapping out again at the next stop. . . . I catch
sight of an outsize jumping winged insect
which brushes my hair
and falls lamely to the floor
beside me, its limbs oddly immobilized,

limp. Another leaps past, settles
on my scalp—my hand brings forth a pink-paper crane,
one of a dozen or more lovely origami birds my girls
have crafted; my son, in turn,

snatching a few and propelling them
like folded paperplane
gliders. The girls are juggling paper octahedrons—
eight-sided balls—calling them balloons . . .

Strangely, I feel myself sinking into the role of object,
impresario no longer, the watcher watched,
the moulder shaped

to purposes not his own. I see myself
reversed, shrunk in a camera lens
slowly telescoping toward me from a few yards
away, the glass face so large I can't find the supposed

head buried behind it,
no way to edge out of the range—hiss-pffft!—
of crossfire: I'm machinegunned
by intense white
fizzle-pops of exploding magnesium.
Next, I'm accosted
from directly below by a small uniformed neuter round-faced

cherub emerging from somebody's defenseless pinched-open
forked legs, foisting a notepad
and pencil into my groin.
He wails and wails for me to sign.

Before my brain can register
the ear-splitting roars
that shake me, I see two small transistor radios
with disproportionately long antennae:
grim imitation rock, all drums and strident brass,
blaring from one; incongruous Mozart symphony,
all squawks and staticky

violin-strumming, from the other. In one
deft motion, I loosen
the duffle's drawcord.
Grasp the aerial-tip of my Sony cassette-recorder.

Slowly extend the shiny silver
tubing upward between my legs, drawing further and further.
Remove the smuggled, squarish machine
from socks and underwear still clinging
to its switches and dials. Insert a long-playing tape plucked
from my hip-pocket.
Commences the mournful schizoid

arpeggios of a Bartok unaccompanied violin sonata.
Sealed off in the Hungarian vibrato's
close embrace, I slide from my left breast-pocket my diamond-
needle-tip pen, and begin to scratch forth my song.

SHAKUHACHI

Three weeks of drill—
        assorted blowing exercises.
    Three weeks to perfect
        a single
clear short toot. Lips cunningly pursed to the flanged

    mouthpiece of the carved,
        thick jointed hollow pipe
    of bamboo: personal,
        intimate
the strange voice of the wood, concealed bird-throats echoing

    in hollow stalks
        slickened erect from the earth
    like reeds, or sawgrass—
        hoarding
secret songs of the wind, whistling for years in cavernous

    tunnels of the wood's
        body. . . . The whole torso a single
    elongated tube-throat
        waiting,
waiting for its rooky trills and wind-primed, stored warbles

    to be released by one pair
        of exquisitely puckered man-lips,
    and skillfully twisted
        fluttering
man-tongue. The sawed-off segment of undying bamboo attuning

    its sapling grace
        and lithe driftwood twists
    to the clasp of one pair
        of hands
fueling the curved bone of its marrowless length with palm-oil

    as gnarled walking stick—
        no mere serviceable cane—
    is nurtured by the handprint's
        whorled
love of its master. Man & slotted pipe. Snake charmer

& hypnotized, stiffened subject.
      A duet with the tailless and tongueless
  operatic serpent.
      Voiceless
mouth which vibrato or tremolo mouths may summon to voice.

III. Two for the Evening Star

TWO FOR THE EVENING STAR

(Improvisations on a theme
from the Japanese of Ryuichi Tamura)

I. THE DAY WHEN THE MERCURY SANK

The day when the mercury
sank, I rose
with the twilight moon
of twenty below zero, climbing

two rickety flights of steps to visit the evening star
of Western poets. The Anglo-American Fuji!
In the East Village, New York,
I mounted the summit

to his upstairs back alley cold water flat slowly enough
to help the rising full moon to help
nameless tottering city skeletons
unbending to lift

thousands of shovelfulls of three-foot-deep
all day's falling moon
snow, sending back fullmoonfall,
sending back

back-hunching bushel throws of fallen moonlight
hopelessly spilling into the gutters,
overflowing into the sunken basement stairwell
I bypassed as I began my halt

tortoise-ascent. I peered
over the banister into the mole's burrow
tunnelling below the tenement entrance. It harbored
a small printer's shop, a law office: the single lightning bolt,

zigzagging vertically down the window, split
the names of three law partners
into unequal cobwebbed shares
of the defunct firm. Two flat boards backed

the cracked pane. *Here, too—eminence perched*
on squalor! I mused, as my footfalls
grew fainter and fainter dimmed by my pulse's thudding
in my pixy-erect ears buried

in vapor blooms of panted breathsteam
exhaled between gulps of the dank thin upperair ether
above the timber line of the tallest
lamppost. . . . *A deer at bay falls from the cliff.*

I wrench my words from the air. The absences
widen.
My poem has a murderous appetite.
Caves in the air

are dying for breath.
I am breathing for death. Breathless.
If a man falls from the cliff
to fill the missing gaps,

did my dream push him
off? The day of our blinding light death
was a black cold day. The nightmoon
whitens. . . . With not one wingbeat, I glided up the second flight

of stairs as if dreaming my weightless body
upward, my arms extended from the wingbones of my shoulders
spanning the passageway, more to stabilize my flight
than to sustain my featherless

soaring. Abruptly, the door swung open.
Back from my raised hand.
My sharp knuckles poised to rap. Left hanging
in naked blunder.

Nowhere to hide. No way
to shelter the frail exposed sparrows' wings
of my open palms: the long slender
plumes of my tapering fingers grew slimmer, narrowed:

I saw as if for the first time their much-touted platform
scrawniness, as they rose and fell,
dwarfed and swaddled in the voluminous pumping
handclasp of my host—

palms lumpish,
knuckles swollen like walnuts.
And it may be I reddened
to the sharp-cornered tips of my high elfin ears

as I stared at the thick puffy barnacles, pendulous,
drooping over his sideburns.
I scanned the poet's room, blank
and bare and square.

A small low stool.
A typewriter on the desk.
A few sheets of a musical score dropped at random—
no surprise to me! A poet's workroom

may hide the stains of his craft.
The studios of painters and sculptors are drenched
with foams and dribblings,
chiselflecks and flakes and scalloped shavings—

gorgeous leftovers! Rainbow
pigeondroppings of tools and materials.
Ambrosias. Cerebral incense. You can brain-smell
aromas of the molding and dissolving

of shapes. With a publicist's hungry eye, I
sleuthed the flat, up and down,
for raw telltale data—
memo jottings:

Black coffee. Dry martini mix.
A Lucky Strike. . . . *Light-years back, in the eyes*
behind my eyes, flashed my Kamakura study:
manuscript papers strewn like fallen autumn leaves,

pages of verse translation in progress, the inherited Chinese
ideograms boldly stratified in vertical columns,
each character a microcosm fiercely announcing its independent
life on the page, I marrying

the towers of Japanese Kanji
to corresponding horizontal chain-links of your English Romaji:
All betrothals! Weddings of tongues, of peoples. . . . I lost the drift
of his English, a maundered syllable-

jumble, and affixed my baffled glare to the opposite wall,
    settling on two wire-hung pictures
bobbing over his right shoulder as, squatting, he shifted
    his weight about on the stool

in rhythm with his discourse:
a watercolor of his mountain chalet—a summer retreat
hugging a forested crag in Austria. An austere portrait
    of E. M. Forster. Ah! Far more

than in all his prattle, the poet loomed
    before me revealed,
    his secret made visible
in his threefold regalia of emblems:

The Forsterian remnant of stalwart Victoriana.
    The pristine Austrian woods.
    The squalid New York
    slum. "I visited

Japan in 1938," he reminisced. "We stayed one hour,
    no more, at Haneda Airport.
From there, I flew straight with Isherwood to China,
    then at war, you'll recall,

with Japan." My face blazed!
Did he mistake my ardor for pain?
    To stop his unguarded mouth,
the poet raised his vast knobby hand to bid me good-bye.

II. PORTRAIT OF THE POET

Today I saw the magazine cover picture of your sixty-fifty-birthday face.
    In the deep fissures of your brow, I traced a map of wars:

canyon-floors flecked with the hoofprints of advancing cavalries,
    the bootprints of stamping infantries;

and in the ravines of your cheeks, more lightly pocked, I deciphered
    the hands-and-knees' prints of trapped and fleeing innocents;

and in those wide crevasses, quartermoon-curves, under your eyes,
    I decoded permanent faults left by facial earthquakes,

the three or four continental shelves of your lower face slipping and
sliding
          against each other, violently grinding their surfaces,

as each fracture in the political earth's crust—each world conflagra-
tion—
          left its imprint in the gulleys of your jaws, the cleft of your chin.

In all those haunted grooves, chiselled and gouged from left to right,
          I read blueprints of history—yours and ours—

          as in the fork-tipped veinwork of leaf-fossils

          as in the creases in a torn-out page of biblical scripture
                    folded and unfolded for thousands of rereadings,
          hidden by day in the underclothes of the atheist's slave

          as in the many-layered cross-section of the crumpled wall
                    of a twelfth-century brickwork shrine, war-ravened
          survivor of twice-a-dozen remortarings and replasterings

          as in stitching and unstitching of immortal lines in a score
                    of manuscript revisions of Yeats's "Sailing to Byzantium"

          as in the workmanlike beveled edges and keenly trained rhymes
                    of your own immortalizing verses to Yeats

          as in the strata and substrata of mineral veins, sedimentary
                    lodes deposited by ancient underground streams
          long since run dry, and now embedded in layered sheets of the
          rock,
                    charting, stratum by mineral-rich stratum,
          the great ages of geologic time

          as in scorched and blackened streaks in the bark of the charred
                    center-beam timbers of a reconstructed Buddhist temple
          bombed-out and incinerated by B-52s in World War II,
                    counter-flames from the unkilled cedar-trunks burning
          outward
          from their life-cores, standing off the flames of TNT

So must your inner-life burning withstand war's omnivorous fire-
storms.
          So bespeaks the burnt-cork-stained wide trenches of your face.

THE BEACON LIGHT OF OSHIMA

(translated from the Japanese of Ryuichi Tamura
with Toshikazu Niikura)

I hate a new house.
Maybe because
I was
Born and brought up in an old house.

There is neither a table to dine with the dead,
Nor minute slits or grooves
For organic burrowers
To inhabit. "The pear tree is split," I wrote in my poem

Twenty years ago or so.
I have planted another pear tree
In the diminutive soil of my garden.
In the morning, I sprinkle water over it.

I wish I could grow death inside the new pear tree.
I wish it could drink itself to death
Out of my hand, living out
Its own green dying.

I wish we could bloom slowly into our own green death.
I wish all day.
At night I read Victorian pornography.
I tell myself I have no illusion about the future.

That is my only illusion. That I have none. Or,
That we have any future. . . .
There goes that flash above the horizon forty kilometers
Out to sea

From my study window:
The beacon light of Oshima
Island. Thirty years old, or so.
Every thirteen minutes, it squelches my thought.

IV. The Izu Peninsula

CAPE IRO: THE STONE PILLARS
(for James Dickey)

I

We follow the switchback trail
    uphill, a slow
      ascent
to the lighthouse—its tower glinting
      overhead. As we mount
    the last
windbreak, sea-spume blasts us
      blindingly . . .
              I gasp
    at the vista!
A dozen-odd great spears of rock,
      upward-pointing, straddle
    the cape.
Strung together, they form a horse-
      shoe curve.
           A row
    of teeth!—
they are petrified fangs, jutting skyward
      from a drowned mastadon's
    lower jaw-
bone, sunken and embedded in offshore
    coral reefs.
           Coastal
    stalagmites!

II

We squint into the scratched eyepiece
    of the motorized
      whirring binoculars,
pulsing on its rock-socketed stem
    (a mammalian
      eye with a heart in it,
throbbing its three-minute panorama). . . .
    Close-up.
      Highest pinnacles
disclose patches of earth, wide heaps
    near the base
      rimming high water mark
stains, a few yards above sea level.

Midway
   up the sleek bare
shafts, thick earth-clumps cling,
   nestlike,
      to ridges of stone;
each, solitary and isolate.
                         (Eagles'
      eyries?
   Not just bloodclots
flecking the mastadon's gums, as my eye'd,
      distantly,
         guessed). . .
                  Uneroded!
Deposits of sea-scum and wave-silt
      balancing
         soil-waste, wash-off
from rain and surf, by an unerring
      symbiosis:
         many trees—tall pine,
cedar, cypress—find lodgement
      in earth-bulbs
         sunk in clefts
deep as tide pools.
                  Potted hothouse
      flora!
   A few aspen scale
peaks of the stone spear-heads (no
      timberline
         in the upper reaches),
scores of gulls and sea-hawks perched
      on tree-limbs
         or gliding aloft. . . .

               III

Geological enigma!
                  Misplaced puzzle
      piece, transplanted
      from the wrong
jigsaw seascape to this low-lying
      headland:
                  peninsula
      tip of few
hills and shallow valleys, coves.

No plunging gorges
   or abysses.
No lofty crags or high mesas to match
    the dozen grim incisors
      of stone. . . .
Twin of the Grand Tetons, Wyoming's
    displaced American
   cousin
to the Swiss Alps—a whole skyline
    of barrens: escarpments,
   summits,
gnarled peaks . . .
               Lacking a Matterhorn!
    How account for so much
   bare rock
in a country of colorful lush Ozarks,
    Smokies, Grand Sierras,
   Big Horns?

              IV

The eyepiece is blinkered, two black
   shutters
     guillotining my view.
Shaken from reverie, I trip.
              Hover
    on cliff-
     ledge. Stabilize. No
guardrails, gates, or low stone walls
    fencing in
      viewers.
            The children—
by leaps and darts—take their turns
    at telescopy,
      racing across rocks, sparse
foilage.
         Gently chiding, I warn them
    to return
     from the lookout viewing
ledge to the pathway, finding the enemy
    in their eyes—
      myself, foe to all
sure-footed impulse.
           They oblige,

veering
    back from the precipice
edging the lookout; then, they sweep
    with one will—
      a cunning nonchalance—
to the adjacent lighthouse.
                            Sidestepping
    the paved
    approach walk, they detour,
sliding freely across loose pebbles, a few
    sharp-edged
    cobblestones, gravel.
Their moves erratic, they skirt
    borders
    of the overhang—sprindrift,
darting hawks and squalling wind fueling
    their wildness. . . .
    In me, outsize panic.
A fear of heights beyond everything.
    I hide
      my eyes—face away.

SHIMODA: THE LAVA SHORES

Three days, too short a late-autumn span of trekking hours
to halve, or quarter, the great pineapple-shaped Izu Peninsula,
   we choose a coastal route:
   of a mind half sea, half land
  (taking a safe middle course, neither mariners nor moun-
   taineers), we follow the chiselled
   features of the land's three-sided
lower face. Cheek by jowl, we scale all lovely shores and shoals
of Izu's jawbone. All earth-life stripped to lineaments. Contours.

Outlines. Edges. We distantly survey the upper bulbous skull-
life, the chain of extinct volcanoes—richly wooded—that bisects
   the long melon of sea-probing
   land, inferring the hidden
  middle segment of the great unbroken range of summits
   extending south into the Pacific,
   a two-hundred-mile-scattering loop
of island volcanoes, the Seven Isles of Izu; and north, beyond Izu,
into the heartland of the Hakone range, abruptly overtopped by Goliath

Fuji's snow-cone, the miracle glacier adrift in the upper second-sea
of stratosphere. . . . We catch hints of the peninsular midsection
   in scraggly lava-rocks: gorgeous
   purply-black free form instant
  sculptures strewn along a quarter-mile of Shimoda's coast-
   line, adjacent to sandy routine
   beach rimming the cliff-base.
What the source (nothing in sight, surely!) of these wantonly scattered
jagged-edged masses, pitted, sponge-pocked; heavy—of high specific

gravity—despite the dilutions of mass by contained air-pockets.
Imagine spongy rock! The prank of a comic deity. Meadows of blackened
   and magically hardened sea-spume,
   solidified foam or froth, ranging
  from pocket-size pebbles to twenty-foot-high boulders. . . .
   A wildness in the form and texture
   of the rocks touches off an urge
in ourselves to unleash all pent-up forces that seek to swirl free
and flow into craggy molds, artifacts of disgorged innards. Who-in-me

fears the sharp cutting edge of brute rock shakes loose from its bonds
and runs naked! My unknown winged body sprints over lava-crowns
   splashing into pools in unforeseen
   gaps and sockets, my ankles
  knowing as never before how not to twist, my hips' vaulted
   broadjumps springing from second
   sets of tendons and ligaments undug
from the tame everyday twins. The children follow, scaling heights
above my orbit, overtaking me; my small son, balancing on the ladder

of my back, catapults to a perch overhead, all my fear for his safety
punctured as the heart of the mountain wafts cold fire through my
breath,
   the ice light of the great snow-cone
   coming on in my eyes: I contain deaths—
  my thousand dyings—in this one fiercely gentle fire-blossom
   leaping of my single whirled-whole
   life. The black glassy rock
takes secret possession of our bodies' reflexes, pulse, glandular
secretions. New hormones bubble up and spit. We snort and growl

with a happiness that sleeps in the soul only lion body can give
but joy no body can surround or contain—awakened, it rolls
   over the musculature, the sheathes
   of under-skin tissue web-work,
  electrifies the skeleton—ah, molten bones!—and sheds
   all slag of flesh, all scoria
   of unillumined joints, lobes, flabs. . . .
We are taking broader leaps, wider side-skips. Unflinching, we skate
on ice-slick wetted expanse, flying into the suck and seethe

of churning high breakers; rounding the Cape, we approach the end
of lava barrens. We climb to a wide high cave indenting the headland
   cliff, turn a corner in the cave-
   mouth and I hear myself yowl
  at the marvel of O'shima's weaving upwards spiral scarf
   of smoke! The live island crater
   exhales a wispy hot perennial breath
in salute to Fuji's everlasting white crown looming in sudden
brilliant silhouette atop a black cloud-mass poised on the horizon.

JOREN: THE VOLCANIC FALLS
(for Ralph Mills)

1. THE DETOUR

No time to ride the tram-car up the precipice
overlooking Shimoda Bay,
   where Commodore Perry flew the first U. S. Consular
flag in Japan . . . No time
                  to read fine print under rocks and sculptures
                     in the Museum of Phalluses,
                        erotica
            masqueraded as art and geological prodigies . . .
            We mill around
            a far-flung central bus stop, junction of bus lines
               to all points
               of the heart-shaped peninsula,
                  north, east or west: a sprawling bus-switchboard
   with dozens of outdoors terminals; behind each,
line-ups of waiting passengers.
   After mistakenly filing in three long rows,
we connect. *Coast Highway closed.*

   We shall detour north up Mt. Amagi, cross Mt.
      Amagi Pass, then transfer
         back to sea-
side. . . . Cruising slowly across the long low valley stretch
         inland from coast
to foothills, we speed up, capriciously, on the first uphill
         curves.
         Wheel-ruts and chuck-holes
   roughen. The driver, rural kinsman to manic
            Tokyo cab jockeys, edges closer and closer
            to the road's Continental-left side,
               which vanishes beneath us.
                           I leer dizzily
            from the left-rear window, hiding
   my winces from the children. How do we find room
      to dodge the occasional
         motorist
bearing down on us from above with no warning on curves?
   No shoulder.

> The moldering
road-edge borders the cliff.
>   What prevents our wheels
>   from sinking,
>   plunging us into the gorge?
>   How is it the driver's bold fast moves

>   negotiate the gravel-run's ducks and swoops.
> I can see a direct plumbline
>   down the precipitous overhang—we are flying!
> *Bite down hard and hard*
> *   on my fear   open me to the exact beauties*
> *   of the live flowing valley*
> *   rippling*
> *   and shimmering   a river of grasses and leaves and tree-tops*
> *   flying below   spilling*
> *   into a long iridescent tunnel of our going   fanning out*
> *   behind us*
> *   streaming away . . . We loop*
> *   a grand circling mountain dance   a spiralling*
> *upsweep:*
> *   bus   road   cliff   valley—*
> *   revolving*
> *and careening all together: no swerves!*
> *The whole valley breathes our heaving and swaying*
> *course—our moves the mountain's breath. . . .*

>   Swoosh!
>   The bus lurches right, bucks,
>   taking a high bounce,
>   rear wheels
> upraised for a full three seconds.
>   My sucked-in breath
>   explodes, the killed road
> rematerializing beneath our axles. Now we are riding
>   flat and level.
>   A conspicuous sign flashes
>   our altitude in meters: the last rise
>   we floated across is the peninsular apogee—
>   Mt. Amagi Pass!
>   We coast,
>   skirting a ridge suspended over a double-crater
>   valley, so densely wooded

I can barely make out in silhouette the family
    of extinct volcanoes that lived
        and died here.
These defunct craters spawn teeming legions of forests,
    mammoth ferns, high grasses,
wildflowers . . .
        The road, narrow ribbon nestled between two
    rows of hills,
        bears a sharp uphill left.
We halt. *Dogashima junction.* The bus empties.

2. THE DESCENT

Three hours stopover. Last bus to West Coast.
Shall we risk the long hike down
    the steep earth-crevasse to Joren Waterfall?
We stroll to the edge of the ravine,
        hover on the upper lip of a downhill trail,
        a serpentining pathway.
        Voices
    approach from below.
        Three slender figures in kimonos—
    two women and a man—
emerge, advancing slowly in a zigzag course up the sheer
    incline;
    one woman, trailing
    the others by a short gap, braces each second
step with a bamboo cane.
        She jerks to a stop.
Eyes shut, hand cupped over her nose,
    she whiffs immense slow breaths—in alternate
snorts—through each nostril, drawing

    silent vast power from the atmosphere. *To breathe*
    is the art . . .
        How far down
    are the falls,
we ask? One hour, the man replies, bowing from the waist.
    We all bow and bow. . . .
Warning the children to follow—not lead!—we descend.
    I test
    each step, noting the irregular
pattern of man-made stone shelves, terraced

ridges, notched and indented in the rock.
I mark the slipperiness of gravel,
         the skid-risk of oblique slopes—stooping,
    my knees close to earth, I stalk,
   grasping rock-knuckles, tree-limbs jutting
      over the path, or latticework
        intertwining
vines and lovely flowering shrubs.
                                 Two rabbits scurry
         underfoot. I trip over one,
trying to snatch the other. Debra spots a fawn, leaping
      from a cliff
      overhead, its white furry tail
vanishing into a small cave-mouth. At last,

   we take turns passing each other on the narrow
single-file path. A wind
   I hardly noticed (fanning gently my left cheek)
shifts and gusts, shoving me
         from behind!
                    How does wind velocity build
         in this gulf, fissure,
            deep earth-
   rent, gouge, rock-enclosed mountain crevasse?
                        I retard
      my steps to a halt too fast,
   lean back on my heels, and crouch to keep from falling.
      The children
         speed up, their heads
      and backs rolling in a downward spiral
   below my legs   disappearing   reappearing
around bends. *Such grace and poise*
   in the rhythmic sweep of wind-lashed limbs!
Beautiful, their absent pitching

   of hips and calves! How lovely the mindless
      unmindful dance I missed,
         too self-
bewitched, caught up in my own dream-gliding trance.
         Surefooted, they caper
and sprint as small animal paws—all weightless ease—
         scuttle.
      In my long ten second
   lapse   space! space!   so much free wideopen
         floating invisible being

                              Oh how I listen!
      I can hear my underfoot heel-
            tapping and small branch crackling die out.
      The wind-whine, tickling my neck,
   quietens, dissolves into a bass two-octave-lower
         sigh-absorbing rumble, ahead
               and below:
a distant gurgle too evenly dinning to be surf washing ashore,
         a sound of water
flying in wide slender sheets, water caught and wailing
         as it spreads
         into a tower of falling churn—
   suds, lather and froth—diffusing to spray

   at the misty perimeters: the falls, the falls!
We draw near to the chasm floor.
   I pursue the runaway children—lunging,
I stumble into a soft gravel bed
            at the foot of the winding path, half-tripping
               into a wide oval pool
                  of dark blue
         water, so shatteringly clear I can see a few sparkly bits
               rotating at depths
         of fifty to a hundred feet: a crater pool—or bottomless
               abyss?—
            many times deeper
            than wide, deeper than the distance around,
   deeper than the steep high whirling wall
of water that empties into its mouth,
   tons of wetness plunging from the canyon
roof, hurtling its body of mountain-top

      apocalypse—a sky-fire-keen howl of downgush!—
         into the serene instant-calm
            of the rippleless
level poolface: the silvery raging belt of churned-up foam
         tearing itself apart, wetness
shattering, ripping itself inside out, eating its heart
            out to become
         scud—weightless, bodiless—
   to fight free of the bonds of mass, gulping
            air-pockets in mouthfuls, feeding on substanceless
         ether, absorbing more and more
            of the floating sun-laced life of bubbles; swindled

by the mountain's lie, the summit's
promise of harvest into airborne vapors, a reward
for falling, falling, falling
to its cease,
exhausting itself in a mighty impact on the pool's stony face . . .
Distrust the lure
of innocent leaps, bounds, hurdles. Fear the trigger-impulse
of the child
within, of the child in all.
Where are the children? Have *they* been whisked,

resistlessly, into the drink?
I cry out, stunned.
The girls—their voices muffled trills—
answer.
They are entombed, locked in the wall
to my left, the gay replies muted,
filtered through thicknesses of volcanic quartz.
Echoing resonances. I leap
across bulrush
to the wall, start to claw the children free from a cliff-grave
with shredding fingernails.
Can their small bodies fit around this bare smooth rock-surface,
slightly arched—
I ponder, tracking with my palms?
The ledge at my feet answers. Two short zigzag
steps across the lip of a shallow cave
glide me into a high long cavern.
I follow the pool-edge trail, a narrow
overhanging ridge, and join the girls—

transfixed by a view beside the falls. Squinting,
I make out dim outlines. *Take*
two steps. Refocus.
At the far end of the basalt cave, I secure ideal sight-access!
Slowly, I translate the placard
posted on the cave-wall:
Buddha-image behind falls named Jizo.
Guardian deity
of small children. Carved
from natural rock by Kobo-Daishi. First Shingon
Buddhist in Japan.
Balancing on the cave-ledge,
we lean over the pool rim to peer

at the lofty fine chisel-work of the priest,
the gentle curvaceous face and shoulders
looming above us from the twenty-foot-high
Divinity carved in shallow
relief,
indenting the rock to varying depths, sunk to a foot or two
in elongated gaps
framing the cheeks (hovering, neckless, over wide shoulders)
and columnar
thick biceps; below,
his delicate turned-in hands resting on cross-

legged lap, the fingers upcurled, knuckles
and thumb-tips of both hands touching,
each to each: in Mudra position, hand-symbol
of sermonizing.
From our perch, the falls
drape the Buddha diagonally, half-blurred
by the shawl of falling
water,
half-clear and distinct.
We try to visualize the brave sculptor-
priest stretching his gaunt
lank-fasted frame slenderer on tip-toe to keep from toppling,
sucked
into torrents of the water-
wall just parallel to his back, and flung
headforemost into the pool-side granite!
Now we see him mounting his makeshift
scaffold of woven osiers and vines, climbing
the wickerwork ladder toward the high

great creaseless forehead and intricate marbly
design of the noble God's
corona.
We see him chopping and battering the wonderful half-shut
eyelids shaped like butterfly
wings, his elbows often grazed by the churning water
behind him—
adjacent to his heaving shoulders
wielding the primitive hammer and stone chisel—
sending a charge of hydroelectric power
into each of his swings.
How happy
he is, the magic voltage of the falls roaring

into his limbs, animating his whole
skeleton with a power like fire—fire born
of water; his slim frame
seems to shed
all remains of flesh, exposing a radiant luminous bone-
tree.
He shudders and quakes
with love-toil, hovers as a candle-flame pants on its wick.
"Kobo-Daishi,
Kobo-Daishi":
his name on my lips,
a gasped murmur, rises to prayerful chant,

the girls winking. (Impish snickers.) I point
to the statue,
"See him there, watch
his swings! Oh how he dances hammer-blows
into the stone, the sparks flying
all around his flushed neck and ears, a galaxy
of flint-sown stars doused
in the falls,
instantly reborn, showering from tireless blows of his stone
hammer, dying out,
born afresh each moment, constellations of fiery pinpoints
of light—
a frenzy of creation!—
circling his voluptuous strokes."
But they
see a different scene, their yelps—barks
of alarm—shattering my spiel.
Their truant brother, the family drifter,
reappears at the Buddha's base.

How did he scale the steep rocky slopes behind
the falls, daring to leap
over a corner
of pool-edge, passing unnoticed by the rear approachway—
surprising us?
Trapped
between rival impulses to scold and warn him, I choke
down my cries,
and sink into the cave-wall
at my back, dazed.
He ignores us, squatting

on the narrow ledge at the statue's foot,
parodies the Divinity's cross-legged
straight-backed posture, the blank stony
stare and half-closed eyelids.
Now he begins
to slip down the slight incline of his roost,
the seat of his pants
and trousers-
legs sliding him toward the perilous junction of falls
and pool.
He tumbles,
half-losing his balance (no hiding the fear in his eyes),
rolls over
on his side, and scrambles
to safety—clenching his sister's outstretched

hand, dancing and cavorting the last few
steps to simulate poise, control.
My hand, open palm flat to the cave-side,
braces my weight. I hold steady,
let the spinning lights slow down behind shut
eyelids, shortness of breath
freezing me
to the spot.
The children's voices fade, thinning
in the distance as they skip
downstream, following the run-off from the pool outlet.
The shaking fit
falters. Quits . . .
Dreamily,
I brush my fingers up and down, from right
to left in widening circles, startled
by the coarse texture of wall,
varying in color from dark gray to black—
thinking, *igneous, igneous rock.*

Fire-begotten. Fire-container. Glassy hardness
repeats my pulse. Wall-rock
thumps
with my stolen heartbeat, my blood flow thudding in stone.
My lifelines—handprint whorls—
fight down terror, finding deep calm in the touch of rock.
When Kobo-Daishi
paused, dreamt between chains

of hammer-blows, he knew this wedding of flesh
  to mountain-rock, this union of opposed
    bodies to make a third, a vessel,
      a medium, a mock-human brooding image:
      the Buddha Ikon:
          a stone body
  inviting the great Spirit of the God to enter,
    to become enshrined, to inhabit
      the stone skull,
stone breast, folded stone limbs—with grace of touch
      the God enchanted by the man
to break holy silence, to rise from the mute invisible
        void and enter
      the avatar of body-form,
    engaging the man in a lordly dance of Spirit:

    the human to be rewarded with eternal grace,
  and grace to all who come after
    by luck to this consecrated place of blessings
  to children: safe passage, safe
          child-passage throughout life . . . Kobo-Daishi, who,
          in caves north of this gully,
            met and fought
      and subdued demons, then sculpted the rock-embossed body
          of the God beside the falls . . .
      Again, I pass my hand across the wall, sweeping from side
            to side. Tall
            wavy columns of basalt rock.
        No lava-slag. No vomitus from the planet bowels
  crater-spewn, leaving blanketed acres of live
topsoil smothered by black dross.
    No formless wild spatter of chunks. No coughed-up
clots of earth-blood . . .
          My palms imbibe

    flaming masses of liquid earth, sudden rivers
      exploding between continental
        shelves
and shaped into wall-forms below the surface, the columns
      jutting closer and closer
to the planet skin, the mountain evolving layer by layer
        from within—
      a struggle to contain
    the swelling pool of fire.

My pulse is afire.
I stroke this chilled rock-face, volcanic
braille, deciphering by touch
the fantastic blaze which melted the earth,
the violent magma-boil tearing
deep cracks in earth's lower crust, molten
fire-rock thrusting upwards,
freezing
in place, quick-set and quick-shaped in formed columns,
earth's fireball center
sculpting and re-sculpting its surface outwards. . . .
Here,

in this place
of change—midway sector,
caught between form and flow, essence

passing between shape and unshapen fluid,
this incision in cliff-side, this mouth,
this great unstanched wound in world's body—
I read the peristalsis of her cycles.
Igneous rock. Fire-born. Fire-swallower.
Quick-melted, quick-set
in the cooling
of its own fires.
Ah!—to contain vast inner fires,
then to be shaped
by effusions and wanings of the flames, riding the wave
of torrential
flow, trapping the blaze
in marbly-veined shapely columns.
My body's
dreamscape! Naked border zone where earth's liquid
core and chilled outer crust meet.
In this place of delicate thresholds, birth
is open wide, the kiss

of deep inner fires still close to the surface—
all transformations! All
fountainings!
Hot spring waters boiling into steams.
Geysers spouting
fumy sprays.
Liquid

rock bursting to the surface, crystallizing into minerals,
        jewels,
    and walls of volcanic
  glass.
        The falls igniting into foam. . . .
            Beachcombers, seaside vagrants, we chose lowland
            peripheries, but uplands chose us,
                wafting us up foothills to summits, luring us
            down into the mountain's innards.
    We voyage into the gash—exposed interior
        of earth's tender Mucosa,
            membranous
lining of her body cavities, her panoramic acreage of rock-
        viscera laid bare. . . .
                    I saunter
down the stream-side path knowing, as never before, earth's
            give-and-take,
            the recoil and snapback
    of gravelly walkway, springy to footfalls.

                    3. THE WHOLE BREATH

    I meet the children dropping hook-and-line
        from handmade bamboo poles
            into the brook,
run-off waters from the falls.
                    Fish strike the small
            breadballs of bait
in midair, leaping from below, their tails kicking up
            little whirlpools
        on the surface.
                    The young men
    who lent the poles, reclining in idle poses,
            applaud, while the children toss their whole catch
            back into the stream—three bucketsful—
            each unhooked fish lively, flapping, uninjured,
        the human sport a brief detour
    in their joyous cycle from mountain-top birth
            to valley streams, riverway
            to the sea.
Here, near the exploding falls, all life-lines between man
        and creature   connect,
connect. Everywhere, the life of water   rock   fish   child
        sweeps

from form to form: glorious
interchange!—the alive of all terrestrial

families nurturing every alive other One   by One
by One   the smashed waters dying
    at the God's foot   issuing forth from the sleep
of the deep crater-pool into child-
                    blessing rivulets: a place of healing!
                            Molten rock
        boiling and burbling upwards
            from below,
    iron-heavy pile-driving waters flung down from the peaks above:
        this atmosphere, each holy
    influx of our dream-breath yawned from the wide free life space
            of Divine
        Breath—opening all around us
        like Mozart's celestial music—is fatefully tinged
    with a fragrance of commingled heights and depths
    a message that passes fiercely from breath
        into mind   held in mind's grip   as volcanic falls
    in aged mountain's memory   are gripped

THE SEA CAVES OF DOGASHIMA

(for Charles and Norma Rogers)

I

We arrive in midday,
by bus. Hefting bags and satchels, we can hardly
stand upright in the wind, great undeflected sea-gusts battering
our flanks. I cannot make out
the landmarks of town,
a blinding hail of fine gravel and dust catching me
full in the face. Lifting
the long wing of my poncho—
a cape to shield my eyes—I cross the highway for views of seacoast.
Hunched at the guardrail, I linger on an elevated
bridge. . . . Before me,

a dense archipelago
of isles and reefs, interspersed by constel-
lations of tiny islets—the larger bodies oddly mushroom-shaped,
puffy and bulbous in the high
middles, eroded and undercut
around the borders. Each ballooning island, shoreless—
a weave of verticals—juts
skyward from the seaface, buoyed
on a sandstone mottled neck just narrower, at the base, than crusts
of overhanging rushes. The mushroom tops
seem to sway

above the stalks—whole
islands teetery over the wasting pedestals,
natural bulwarks lifting them free from heavy swells and pounding
surf. Each upraised land mass,
teeming with birds and foliage
(its luminous silhouette delicately etched on the mist),
flickers and flutters in the cross-
currents of transverse wind gusts.
Now shimmering in the silver-blue haze and rose-glow opalescence
of twilight, the great inverted chandeliers,
endlessly branching,

scatter radiance beyond
measure—each island, a mirror-image of the town
upborne . . . Dogashima.

Town on stilts!
Undulant city, rocking
on trestles!
Population adrift
on a boardwalk-wharf, quay of stone blocks and knotty
planking: a floor to the town,
to beach, a slatted roof. Dozens
of long sloped ladderways connect shore to village, ranging from one
to four flights as the Coast falls away, slants
into the horizon.

II

Several ferries,
sighted from the small balcony of our private
ryokan overlooking the beach, circle Dogashima Bay—dawn to dusk,
each follows the same deft route,
a zigzagging switchback course.
Three craft in view, each at a different phase in the winding
seaways labyrinth, negotiate
intricate sharp turns and arcs
through straits between islets, or narrow canals into sea-caves,
tunnels bisecting natural rock cathedrals.
The small vessels,

queerly vanishing
into the hidden sides of apparently solid
rock-knolls, beetle out the opposite end, moments later. Or they emerge,
startlingly, from the entrance—
exiting bow first. They maneuver
with the adroit surety of a team of one-engine skywriter
biplanes swooping into cloud-banks
between words. . . . High caves, notched
like windows, fleck one island's peak. A gull, swiftly cruising, pierces
the slotted apex—fleet passage through the stone
pinnacle's needle eye!

III

A short step down—
we file, bouncily, from dock to upper deck
at midship, the children spluttering *arigatos*, rudely bypassing
the proffered helping hands
and ceremonious bows of kimono-
draped fellow passengers . . . I descend in a babble
of apologies—ours and theirs—
rival choruses, spanning
whole octaves on the melodic flute-scales of Japanese politeness.
Reciting forms colloquial and elegant,
by turns, I spin about

on my heels too late
to scold the children nimbly dancing
along narrow ledges—two on portside, a third on starboard—
approaching the forecastle, swaying
rashly over the oil-blanketed
water as I fantasize leaping overboard for the rescue.
The monkeys, snickering at my shouts,
land safely on a loose plank-seat
high in the bow (hardly a bench!), flanking the shipmaster. I,
withdrawing aft, fall into a low proper seat. . . .
The multitude follow

the skipper into the glass-
enclosed cabin, below. *Do they desert the choice*
deck-quarter to escape a demented foreigner, father to harebrained
louts?. . . . Chugging from the pier,
we take a wide arc to center
of the inlet mouth—the one wide stretch of waterway
in sight uncheckered with land-
shapes. Skipper cuts the engines . . .
Two masked heads, surfacing, dart into view off starboard. We all sweep
astern to witness the men lobbing the large
oval spiralled shells,

tinselled with seamoss,
into the floating bucket. I time the next dive—
two minutes! The master divers, sporting ageless physiques, haul in
scores of prized *awabi*, hourly,
from seafloor rock-shelves
one hundred feet below. Lifted over those muscly shoulders

for overhand tosses into the wide-
rimmed barrels, the abalone
shells' mother-of-pearl lips flash milky iridescence in the sun. . . .
Picking up speed, suddenly, we enter a maze
of narrow passageways

between countless low-
lying oblongs and a few large humpbacked raised
muffin shapes, marshy and lush. We accelerate, again, churning directly
into a floating skull-shaped edifice
of sheer unbroken stone, void
of all vegetation. It raises its vast protuberant brow
higher and higher over us,
casting its ghostly elongated
shadow across the prow and spreading aft as we approach, never
veering from our collision course. The whole ferry,
at last, is swallowed

in suffocating blackness. Now
we are standing still, the billowing rock-face
charging toward us, its bulging forehead bearing down from above. . . .
Almost too late, we swerve right
and slacken our speed; gliding
around a narrow projecting lip, we follow the perimeter
of the island's base—just beyond
the bend, a great wide mouth opens
above us, yawning over our heads, and we come about, retarding
to a slow sputtery putt-putt. Then we steer
into an apparently boundless

cavity—a geode's hollow?—
expanding between rocky jaws of the island . . .
a moment of grim darkness followed by a play of lights and shadows
on cave-walls of a widening tunnel.
The reversed funnel-shape opens
into a colorful display of greens, yellows, grays: a light-
show flashing on the walls and ceiling
of a natural amphitheater—or chapel!
What the source? The water below, refracting light from distant star-
coral reefs? Or portholes in the rock, hidden
from view, but admitting

fat rivers of light
like projected beams, unstoppable and piercing,
of a high-powered searchlight—lightstreams hurled into the cavern,
tossed back and forth between walls
of the tabernacle, and dispersed,
burying the source? . . . We drift, pivoting, and arrive,
slowing to a halt in the center
of a wide circular pool. Storms
of light—a sudden amazing brightness!—pour down on our upturned
faces. We stare directly overhead into an oval
hole gouged like an eye

of Gargantua clear through
the island cave's stone roof, exposing a naked
ellipse of cloudless sky. Many long vines, tendrils and creepers
of ivy, are suspended like eels
dangling from the rim (a wild growth
of lashes from the giant's lower eyelid). Now the eye
begins to turn, slowly, a clockwise
spinning—I hear twin motors
perk up, rumbling, and I know it is ourselves in motion, again,
revolving in place about a fixed axis, stationary
under the peephole

zenith. Flaming sun
pops into the gap, a fiery white-hot pupil
crossing from left to right. I stare at the flower of fire, squinting.
The blossom sends forth flares
of bloom, unbearably bright flame-
tongues, radiating outwards from the center. As quickly,
it dances away—smarting our eyes
like a solar eclipse (no time
to flinch), then leaving us to blink away intense pained after-images
exploding under our shut eyelids: Roman
candles spouting balls

and stars of fireworks.
Shading my eyes, I peer through narrowest
eye-slits. Two large insects, at opposite corners of the giant eye,
rotate around the edge. From one,
a spiderlike arm unbends, dropping
a small morsel toward us trailing a long twine—it splashes
into water adjacent to our craft.

The other waves an appendage,
as if in greeting. My son waves back. *The view unblurs:* two schoolboys,
leaning over the rock-orifice, dangle bait
from long drop lines

for fish. Grown inured
to the befuddled upturned eyes of ferried
tourists, as to the angry grunts and scowls of the ferrymen, the anglers
melt away into the rock-roof,
their arms and legs blended amid
wind-tossed ivy tentacles. . . . Exiting the sea-cave, we swing
wide to make way for the next ferry—
stealing a single backward
glance: the boys, now straddling the island peak's sunlit crown-fire,
wave farewell, flapping carp-pennants
overhead in the wind.

ABOUT THE AUTHOR

Laurence Lieberman has been widely anthologized; his poems
and critical essays have appeared in most of the country's
leading magazines—The New Yorker, The Atlantic, Harper's,
and The Hudson Review among them. The poetry editor for
University of Illinois Press, he is the author of two previous
books of poetry, The Unblinding (1968) and The Osprey
Suicides (1973) and a collection of essays on contemporary
American poets, Unassigned Frequencies: American Poetry in
Review (1964–77). He is a Professor of English at the
University of Illinois, where he was awarded a creative
writing fellowship by the Center for Advanced Study in 1971,
and spent a year traveling in Japan with his wife and three
children. Most of the poems in God's Measurements, based on
the experiences of that year of travels, explore Japan.